FINDING OUT ABOUT HOLIDAYS

Thanksgiving Day
A Time to Be Thankful

Elaine Landau

Enslow Publishers, Inc.

40 Industrial Road	PO Box 38
Box 398	Aldershot
Berkeley Heights, NJ 07922	Hants GU12 6BP
USA	UK

http://www.enslow.com

Copyright © 2001 by Elaine Landau.

Library of Congress Cataloging-in-Publication Data

Landau, Elaine.
Thanksgiving Day—a time to be thankful / Elaine Landau.
     p. cm.
Includes bibliographical references and index.
ISBN 0-7660-1572-6
1. Thanksgiving Day—Juvenile literature. 2. United States—Social life and customs—
Juvenile literature. [1. Thanksgiving Day. 2. Harvest festivals. 3. Holidays.] I. Title.
GT4975 .L35 2001
394.2649—dc21
     00-010908

Printed in the United States of America

10 9 8 7 6 5 4 3 2

To Our Readers:
We have done our best to make sure all Internet addresses in this book were active and appropriate when
we went to press. However, the author and the publisher have no control over and assume no liability for
the material available on those Internet sites or on other Web sites they may link to. Any comments or
suggestions can be sent by e-mail to comments@enslow.com or to the address on the back cover.

Photo Credits: American Stock/Archive Photos, pp. 15, 20, 36; Archive Photos, pp. 3, 12, 13, 14, 24,
26, 27, 45, 46; Photo Disc, Inc., © 1999, p. 17; © Corel Corporation, pp. 2, 4, 5, 6, 8, 10, 11, 19, 21,
23, 29, 30, 34, 35, 39, 40, 47; Courtesy Harry S Truman Library, *Dictionary of American Portraits,
Dover Publications,* Inc., 1967, p. 38; Engraved by John C. Buttre from a photograph by Mathew
Brady, *Dictionary of American Portraits*, Dover Publications, Inc., 1967, p. 28; Enslow Publishers,
Inc., p. 42; Hemera Technologies, Inc., 1997–2000, pp. 1, 9, 16, 18, 33 (both); Hulton Getty/Archive
Photos, p. 41; Lambert/Archive Photos, pp. 7, 22; Painting by John Trumbull, Courtesy Henry Francis
de Pont Winterthur Museum, *Dictionary of American Portraits*, Dover Publications, Inc., 1967, p. 25;
Reuters/Jeff Christensen/Archive Photos, pp. 31, 32; Reuters/Rickey Rogers/Archive Photos, p. 37;
Skjold Photographs, p. 43.

Cover Photo: © Corel Corporation (background); American Stock/Archive Photos (middle inset);
© Corel Corporation (top and bottom insets).

CONTENTS

Turkey dinner is something that many people look forward to on Thanksgiving Day.

CHAPTER 1

A Special Day

Each year, on the last Thursday in the month of November, people all over the United States celebrate Thanksgiving. It is a special time for families and friends to come together and give thanks.

Turkey . . . stuffing . . . cranberries . . . pumpkin pie. These foods make us think of a holiday. But you probably did not think of St. Patrick's Day or Valentine's Day. These are Thanksgiving Day treats.

We celebrate Thanksgiving every year on the last Thursday of November. It is a special day for many reasons. Friends and family come together. Some people travel many miles to be together. They enjoy good food and good times.

On the Fourth of July there are fireworks. Trick-or-treating is popular on Halloween. But on Thanksgiving Day everyone looks forward to the meal. In most homes it is a busy time for the cook.

Many Americans eat turkey on that day. About 45 million pounds of turkey are eaten every Thanksgiving. With it, we have 65 million pounds of sweet potatoes and 80 million pounds of cranberries. For dessert, 55 million pumpkin pies are served.

Thanksgiving has been celebrated in America for over three hundred fifty years. It began as a harvest festival. After a hard winter, the early settlers known as Pilgrims had a good harvest of many crops. They celebrated with a feast. That is why we think of Thanksgiving as an American holiday.

Actually, people have always celebrated good harvests. This is true around the world. Some of these celebrations date back to long

Pumpkin pie is a popular dessert that many people eat on Thanksgiving Day.

Early settlers known as Pilgrims celebrated the first Thanksgiving as a way to give thanks for a good harvest with many crops.

People from many different cultures have celebrated good harvests for many years.

ago. The names and dates may be different, but the idea behind them is the same.

The ancient Romans had a harvest feast. It was held in early October. They gave thanks to Ceres, the corn goddess. The holiday was known as Cerelia. That is where the word cereal comes from. A wonderful feast would be prepared. There was also music, parades, and games.

The Chinese celebrated good harvests, too. Thousands of years ago they held a three-day Moon Festival. Roast pig and harvest fruits were served. There were small round cakes and candies. The candies were yellow and looked like the full moon.

Jewish people also have a harvest festival. It

is called Sukkoth. Sukkoth began over three thousand years ago. It is still celebrated every autumn. Some families build a small hut made of tree branches for the festival. Leaves are spread over the roof of the hut. Apples, grapes, corn, and other vegetables are hung inside the hut. The festival lasts eight days. But the first two nights are special. On those nights, families eat dinner in the hut. American Jews may celebrate both Sukkoth and Thanksgiving.

Thanksgiving is a time for all Americans to feast and to give thanks. Many families begin their Thanksgiving meal with a prayer. Others attend a religious service that day. They think about all the things for which they are grateful.

People start preparing for Thanksgiving

People all over the world celebrate and give thanks for good harvests.

Thanksgiving is a time for all Americans to feast and to give thanks.

Day weeks ahead of time. Some use old family recipes. Often favorite dishes are served. On Thanksgiving, many people eat more than usual. It is okay to have some extra stuffing or a second slice of pie. It is almost expected. But Thanksgiving is much more than an extra slice of pie. It is about appreciating American life.

Many people use old family recipes for Thanksgiving dishes.

11

A group of people known as the Pilgrims arrived in Plymouth, Massachusetts, in 1620.

CHAPTER 2
The First Thanksgiving

We know what Thanksgiving is like today, but how did it start? The holiday dates back to a special feast that took place long ago.

Thanksgiving began in Plymouth, Massachusetts, in 1620. A group of people known as Pilgrims had just arrived from England. The Pilgrims hoped to lead a life devoted to God in a new land. But first, they had to build a place to live, and that would not be easy.

Their trip from England was also not easy. On

September 16, 1620, the Pilgrims set sail on a small ship named the *Mayflower*. The voyage was long and cold. There were rough storms at sea. The passengers were often seasick. One man died.

Their first months in America were even worse than the voyage. The Pilgrims arrived in

The Pilgrims set sail from England on a small ship called the *Mayflower*. The trip was long and cold, and there were storms.

December. It was a very cold winter, and they did not have enough food. Many Pilgrims became ill and some of them died. One hundred two people had sailed on the *Mayflower*. By spring, just fifty-seven of them were alive.

The town of Plymouth Rock, Massachusetts, as it looked in 1867.

The Pilgrims refused to give up. They tried to plant crops from seeds they had brought from England. But the seeds would not grow in the rocky soil.

These settlers were also not used to catching or hunting for their food. They did not know how to track a deer or where to find the best fish. But then help came.

The Pilgrims had seen American Indians near their village, but the Pilgrims had not spoken to them. That changed on Friday, March 16, 1621. An American Indian named Samoset came to their village. He greeted them saying, "Welcome, Englishmen." The Pilgrims were very surprised to learn that Samoset spoke English. He had learned the language from English fishermen who came to America each year to fish.

Samoset spoke with the Pilgrims. He knew the area well. There had been an Indian village there, but it had been wiped out by disease. Samoset returned a few days later. This time, he brought a friend named Squanto. Like Samoset, Squanto also spoke English.

Squanto helped the Pilgrims. He stayed with them for several months. Their new Indian friend knew which crops would grow. Squanto gave the Pilgrims seeds for corn,

This is what the *Mayflower* might have looked like. This copy of the ship is in Massachusetts.

squash, and pumpkins. Other vegetables were planted too. He taught them to bury a dead fish wherever they planted seeds. This fed the soil and helped the plants to grow.

Squanto took the Pilgrims into the forest. The men learned to hunt for deer, rabbits, and wild turkeys. Squanto also taught them to make good use of the waters in the area. Before long, the Pilgrims were trapping lobsters and digging for clams.

The women and children gathered wild fruits and berries. They learned which were good to eat and which were poisonous. The Indians had used herbs and plants as medicines for a long time. Now, the Pilgrims used them, too.

The Pilgrims might not have survived that first year without Squanto's help. But with it

The women and children learned to gather wild fruits and berries.

Squanto taught the Pilgrims how to hunt for deer.

they succeeded. By fall 1621 the Pilgrims had a rich harvest. There was enough food for the coming winter. They decided to celebrate with a feast.

William Bradford was the Pilgrims' governor. He invited Squanto to the feast.

The Pilgrims shared a day of feasting with the American Indians to thank the Indians for all their help.

Governor Bradford also told Squanto to bring some friends. To the Pilgrims' surprise, ninety Indians showed up. They did not come empty-handed, though. The Indians brought five deer, so there was plenty of food for everyone.

The foods they ate that day are not what many of us eat at Thanksgiving today. There was venison (deer) that the Indians brought and wild turkey. The Pilgrims hunted rabbits, ducks, and geese, which were probably also served. Eel, codfish, sea bass, and clams were probably other foods at the feast.

There was no pumpkin pie. The Pilgrims' supply of flour had run out. While they had no cakes or cookies of any kind, they did eat boiled pumpkin, wild fruits, and berries.

The Indians brought turkeys with them to eat at the very first Thanksgiving.

The boy and girl in this old-fashioned Thanksgiving picture cannot wait to eat the turkey their mother cooked.

No one knows exactly the days when the feast took place, but it was probably sometime in mid-October. The feast lasted three days. The women cooked the food over outdoor fires. Everyone ate outside at long tables. The Pilgrims and the Indians played games. There were footraces, too. The Pilgrims showed off their skills with a musket, a type of gun. The Indians did the same with a bow and arrow.

The Pilgrims enjoyed the feast. But they did not think of it as a time for giving thanks. To them, giving thanks meant hours of prayer and fasting, not eating.

The harvest feast was not held every year. Some years crops failed and there was little reason to celebrate.

Yet, people liked the idea of Pilgrims and Indians sharing a feast. Over time, this harvest feast came to be known as the first Thanksgiving.

Over time, the idea of a harvest feast came to be known as the first Thanksgiving.

The Pilgrims gave thanks
for their safe landing.

CHAPTER 3

The Making of a Holiday

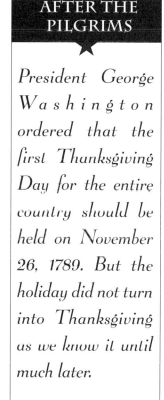

President George Washington ordered that the first Thanksgiving Day for the entire country should be held on November 26, 1789. But the holiday did not turn into Thanksgiving as we know it until much later.

For many years there was no official Thanksgiving Day. Other New England colonies heard about the Pilgrims' harvest feast. Some had their own Thanksgiving celebrations. But those feasts did not take place every year, and no special dates were set.

During the American Revolution, when the American colonies fought for freedom from English rule, several days were set aside for giving thanks. These days were usually after important victories. The first Thanksgiving Day for the entire country, however, was not until

November 26, 1789. President George Washington ordered it, but the custom did not catch on.

In time, some states started their own Thanksgiving Day. New York was one of the first states to do so. By 1817, Thanksgiving was celebrated every year in New York. Other northern states did the same thing. Virginia was the first southern state to follow their lead. Thanksgiving Day became a state holiday there in 1855. The holiday was usually celebrated in November, but different states held it on different days.

People seemed not to see the need for a national Thanksgiving Day. But one woman did not feel this way. Her name was Sarah Josepha Hale.

Sarah Josepha Hale thought Thanksgiving should be celebrated all over the United States.

She is sometimes known as the "mother" of Thanksgiving.

Hale was a magazine editor. Every fall she filled her magazine with Thanksgiving stories, songs, and recipes.

Hale thought that Thanksgiving should be celebrated throughout the United States. So she began writing letters to governors and presidents. Support for her idea began to grow.

After many years Hale's work paid off. In 1863, President Abraham Lincoln declared a day of Thanksgiving for the whole country. It was set on the last Thursday of November. Every president after Lincoln did the same. This custom continued for seventy-five years.

Thanksgiving is a time for people all over the United States to give thanks.

In 1863, President Abraham Lincoln declared a day of Thanksgiving for the whole country.

In 1939, President Franklin D. Roosevelt changed the holiday to the third Thursday of November. This was a week earlier than usual. The president wanted to help American businesses. He hoped making the holiday earlier would make the Christmas shopping season last longer.

But, the public did not like the idea of moving the holiday. People were not sure when to celebrate Thanksgiving Day. Some tried the new date. Others celebrated when they always had. Still others celebrated on both days.

Congress finally set things straight in 1941. Thanksgiving Day was declared a federal holiday. This means the United States government said it was an official holiday. The date was changed back to the last Thursday in

November. On that day all government offices are closed. So are schools, banks, and most businesses. There is no mail delivery. In homes throughout the nation, people celebrate the day and give thanks.

The United States government said that Thanksgiving was an official holiday in 1941.

29

Many people enjoy watching parades on Thanksgiving Day.

CHAPTER 4

A Time for Eating ...and More

Thanksgiving is a feast day, but people often do more than eat. Many enjoy watching Thanksgiving Day parades. Some of the larger parades are in New York City, Detroit, Houston, and Philadelphia.

The best-known parade is in New York City. It is Macy's annual Thanksgiving Day parade. Millions of Americans watch it on television each year.

The parade has marching bands and clowns. There are also huge balloons filled with helium, a gas that is lighter than air. It allows the giant

Marching bands, clowns, and balloons, like Garfield the Cat and Spiderman, are all part of New York's Thanksgiving Day parade.

balloons to float high above the crowds. The balloons are shaped like well-known cartoon and storybook characters. Favorites include Snoopy and Felix the cat.

For some people who live nearby, there is a special treat. The fun starts the night before the parade. They can watch the Thanksgiving Day balloons being filled with helium. It is exciting to see the different characters take shape.

Just like they were for the Pilgrims and the Indians, sports games are still part of Thanksgiving.

The Pilgrims and American Indians ran races at their Thanksgiving feast. There were games, too. Sports are still an important part of Thanksgiving Day today. Football games are especially popular. High school teams play against one another. Some families like playing touch football in their yards.

Americans also watch football on television on Thanksgiving Day. Two National

Football games have become just as much a part of an American Thanksgiving as turkey and pumpkin pie.

Football League (NFL) teams host holiday games. They are the Detroit Lions and the Dallas Cowboys. Many people eagerly look forward to these games. They have become a part of an American Thanksgiving.

But not everyone watches or plays football on Thanksgiving. Footraces are fun, too. That is how many Texans in Dallas begin the holiday. They take part in the YMCA's Turkey Trot. More than twenty thousand people run in the race. Then they head home for Thanksgiving dinner.

The Run for Diamonds is held every Thanksgiving as well. It is a nine-mile race in Berwick, Pennsylvania. There are many wonderful prizes. The top seven

Many towns hold running races as a part of their Thanksgiving Day celebrations.

male runners get diamond rings. The top seven female runners get diamond pendants. Other races are held in many towns and cities. The prizes vary. Sometimes winners get dessert. They can take home a pumpkin or a pecan pie.

One Thanksgiving Day race held in Minneapolis, Minnesota, has a special twist.

Soup kitchens help to feed hungry people in need every day. On Thanksgiving Day, a special meal is served.

The Northwest Athletic Club's run helps the whole community. Runners enjoy the holiday race, but something more important also goes on. Throughout the whole month of November, club members bring food to ten places throughout the city. On Thanksgiving morning, the food is loaded onto trucks and taken to a food bank. A food bank is a place where food is collected and stored. From there, it is given out to people who need it.

These men are being served in a soup kitchen in the 1930s. Soup kitchens feed the homeless and hungry all year, but they are especially busy on Thanksgiving Day.

Others have also tried to make a difference on Thanksgiving. In Harrisburg, Pennsylvania, community groups work together to give turkeys to hundreds of needy families. Similar projects take place in other areas.

Soup kitchens feed the homeless and hungry all year, but they are especially busy on Thanksgiving Day. Many host special holiday dinners. Usually volunteers spend the day helping. They cook and serve the food and clean up afterward. Often the volunteers are students. They help give others a reason to be thankful and experience the true meaning of this holiday.

Everyone deserves a wonderful Thanksgiving. But the holiday is never much fun for turkeys. That is why every Thanksgiving Eve the president of the United States pardons one very lucky turkey. This fortunate bird never reaches a dinner table. Instead, it goes to a Virginia

Harry Truman was the first president of the United States to save one lucky turkey from being eaten on Thanksgiving.

petting farm. It remains there for the rest of its life. This custom began over fifty years ago. President Harry Truman started it. The presidents who came after him have continued to follow this custom.

The turkey that is saved leaves town. Many people also go away for Thanksgiving. Some people visit family and friends, others go to different places. On the day before

Every year one turkey gets a presidential pardon and goes to a petting farm.

Thanksgiving Day is one of the busiest travel days of the year. Many people go away to visit family and friends.

Thanksgiving, airports and highways are often crowded. It is the busiest travel day of the year.

There are many interesting Thanksgiving vacation spots. One is the Ozark Folk Center in Mountainview, Arkansas. There, you can see how mountain people once lived. It is fun to watch a blacksmith work or learn how cider is made from apples. On Thanksgiving Day a special meal is served. Then, there is a Thanksgiving Gospel Concert.

Another great Thanksgiving stop is Plimoth Plantation near Plymouth, Massachusetts. The plantation looks just like the Pilgrims' village. Actors dress and act as the early settlers and Indians did.

It is good to step back into history. We can

Actors and actresses reenact a scene as it might have been during the time of the Pilgrims.

After months of travel at sea, the Pilgrims reached land. They named their new home New Plymouth.

learn how Thanksgiving Day was once celebrated. But trying new things is important, too. Thanksgiving Day is about being grateful. It is also about caring. Challenge yourself this Thanksgiving. See how many ways you can show these feelings. You will be creating your own Thanksgiving traditions.

Thanksgiving is all about giving thanks and being caring.

Thanksgiving Day Craft Project

★

Turkey Seating Cards

After you help set the dinner table, help to set the holiday mood with these seating cards to tell everyone where to sit. You will need:

✔ **brown wrapping paper or a brown paper bag cut open**

✔ **a pencil**

✔ **red, orange, and yellow crayons or markers**

✔ **safety scissors**

1. Place your hand on the paper.

2. Spread your fingers apart.

3. Trace the outline of your hand and fingers. Your palm is the turkey's body. Your fingers are its feathers. Your thumb is its head.

4. Color the feathers red, orange, and yellow.

5. Write a person's name on the turkey's body.

6. Cut out the outline.

7. Be sure to make one for each person at dinner. Place a turkey seating card on the table in front of each seat.

*Safety Note: Be sure to ask for help from an adult, if needed, to complete this project.

Words to Know

★

custom—The way a group of people does something.

editor—A person who corrects written work for a magazine or a book.

fasting—To go without food.

harvest—To gather crops.

pendant—A charm or locket to put on a necklace.

Pilgrims—A group of English settlers who founded the colony of Plymouth, Massachusetts, in 1620.

tradition—To do something the same way each time it is done.

venison—The meat of a deer.

Reading About

Arnosky, Jim. *All About Turkeys*. New York: Scholastic, 1998.

Burckhardt, Ann. *Pumpkins*. Mankato, Minn.: Bridgestone Books, 1996.

Corwin, Judith. *Thanksgiving Crafts*. Danbury, Conn.: Franklin Watts, 1995.

George, Jean Craighead. *The First Thanksgiving*. New York: Philomel Books, 1993.

Miller, Marilyn. *Thanksgiving*. Austin, Tex.: Raintree Steck-Vaughn Publishers, 1998.

Roop, Peter and Connie Roop. *Let's Celebrate Thanksgiving*. Brookfield, Conn.: Millbrook, 1999.

West, Robin. *My Very Own Thanksgiving: A Book of Cooking and Crafts*. Minneapolis, Minn.: Carolrhoda Books, 1993.

Internet Addresses

★

An American Thanksgiving for Kids and Families
<http://www.night.net/thanksgiving/>

Kids Domain Thanksgiving Games
<http://www.kidsdomain.com/games/thanks.html>

Not Just for Kids!
Thanksgiving Fun
<http://www.night.net/thanksgiving/fun.html-ssi>

Nuttin But Kids Thanksgiving Page
<http://www.nuttinbutkids.com/thanksgiving
.html>

Index

★